19 YEARS OF SKIN

KENYA STERLING

Published by Superbia Books
an imprint of
Dog Horn Publishing
45 Monk Ings
Birstall
Batley
WF17 9HU
doghornpublishing.com

This publication and the Young Enigma chapbook competition were supported by a grant from Superbia at Manchester Pride
manchesterpride.com
superbia.org.uk

Writer development, performance workshops and touring funded by Commonword
cultureword.org.uk

Part of Young Enigma,
supporting young and emerging LGBT writers
in the North West of England
youngenigma.com

Edited and designed by Adam Lowe
adam-lowe.com

SECTION 1:

CHILDHOOD

I visited my childhood last night.
You were there.
You told me you'd take me to see the stars.

BENEATH YOU

I unearthed your roots
with dirt-marked skin.
Still roots clung as
the seeds grew in my chest.

A sunflower began to bloom,
petals came into view.
Ripped through.
Tore them off.

He loves me.

He loves me not.

KALEIDOSCOPE

I remember exactly what it was like. The biggest thing you had to worry about was what was on the menu for tea. Fish fingers and beans, or hoops on toast. I never was a beans kid, maybe that was the moment I knew I was growing up - hoops gone - beans on toast it was. Adult life. But childhood is just a dream away for me. A memory. Not too far gone. I have always questioned how I didn't end up with severe health conditions as a kid. My primary school wasn't exactly the most health aware institution. Seconds - thirds - fourths - of greasy, deep fried food. Greasy food and clear skin. Clear as a summer day with the smell of warm concrete and dirt in the air. Running away from Year 6's in the yard. Back when the bigger kids had power. The bigger kids were bolder and didn't think twice about knocking you over in a game of British bulldog. We were just below the threshold of strong and important in Year 3. Slap bang in the middle of the beginning and the end of all that was beautiful and free. It was a year full of belly laughs and snot dripping from noses as we ran from class to class. I think Year 3 was the year I was good at maths and bad a Literacy. It usually switched itself around each year - funny when I think about it now. Everything had some sort of possibility. And I mean everything. Happiness ran through and through. The biggest question you asked was 'Can I play' sometimes followed by an awkward grinning sort of 'It's not my game'. But in those days we knew that was okay. You just found the person who's game it was, and the next thing you knew you were involved. It isn't that easy now. You can't just be involved. Adulthood comes with external pressures, and judgement. You can't just be you. The true authentic version of yourself. You have to be a hundred different versions to the different groups of people you encounter. Each version hoping as much as the other that they'll like you. Hoping they'll ask you to be involved. Low self esteem and persistent suicidal thoughts - or tendencies, depending on which professional you ask. But it's not all bad, that's after you get past the taxes, bills, food and basic living requirements. Then you can enjoy the minimal time to live. The minimal time to breathe. When's the last time you took a deep breath? When's the last time you played? I'm talking about doing a non-directional activity, with no outcome, deadline or expectation.

When's the last time you did something without a purpose? And I'm not just talking to you office workers. I'm talking to you arty farty cunts too. When's the last time you sat in a studio and did something for you? Not for your BA degree, or for a show your involved in. For you. Being an adult can mean losing you. Nothing is sacred or yours. You've got to pump it through 10 filters and post it to tell everyone what a great time your having being 'you'. Childhood never had that did it. Never had some bullshit excuse. You could be everything and nothing and be perfectly perfect all at once. At least, that's my experience. Don't get me wrong it wasn't all fairy dust coming out my arse. But it was one of the only sections of my life where I felt good enough. These days I rarely feel good enough for anything. Finding myself consciously and consistently wondering what my purpose is. Sometimes I look to salvage those memories. Some days I'll choose spaghetti hoops over a tin of beans.

THE TRUTH

I didn't want to do this because I knew.
I wish I hadn't tried to change you.
You take back the typewriter.
I lay my head on your chest because vulnerable.
You deserved better.

LIVE AND LET'S DANCE

Something amazing happened last night and there weren't any drugs this time to to make it happen you know, just a great feeling which poured from my chest it was mad like really mad I don't think I've ever felt something so so so (tries to find the words) intense and I know I'm shit with words but that's what it was like... Intense I was dancing and it was well, it was everything it's all that mattered in that time feeling this music flow through me and I didn't need drugs to do that and I'd had barely any alcohol maybe one or two drinks so this was me, this was all me and even the music wasn't what I usually listen to but after a while I felt what everyone else felt like I couldn't resist the energy around me, I started to embody all that I am as a person like every single second of me was flowing through this this this movement- and dancing it's like another language like a different way to communicate. (Breathe) Goes back to that thing doesn't it primal mating call all that stuff and I'm not saying it always has to be sexual I'm just saying that's where it comes from well I think that's where it comes from and he drew me in for all the wrong primal reasons, it was his awkward dancing that got me it made me realise you can express whatever you want there's no censor or restriction like language, with language there are only a limited number of words in the dictionary but with movement there's so much more you can say so there we are me and him in forty two's and I remember exactly what I said I told him (breathe) 'it's 'in the hips'. I wasn't grafting him. But then there we were. Hands feeling for skin, feeling for the sake of feeling. Everywhere you know. Hips. Back. Neck. Waist. Arse. Grabbing for something. Touching. Feeling. It was like opium. Injecting myself with his hands across my body, whilst amongst us the sweat was rife, and he and I were moving. It was gripping. I could feel burning like like radiating between us. Close. Closer. Me and you our hips collided and there was friction our bodies aligned perfectly the same rhythm of movement we were closer than ever nose to nose, eye contact, locked into each other's gaze whilst also this movement was going on around us a blurry background mess but we didn't notice at all and my vision started to get blurry from it all and I swear when we kissed it was the first time I'd felt such a heavy weight of euphoria and I'm pretty sure that's the right word for it... I was completely bliss an absolute sense of happiness and I was okay that he took that snapshot of my life because his still image still remains and at that time I had complete clarity and control of who I was all of that contained in minutes of kissing to David Bowie's Let's Dance. And we did just that we danced and we sealed it with something special. I'm not sure if any of that made sense… But I just needed to tell someone that something amazing happened last night. Because it did.

CANVAS

Transparent, as you see through my existence.
You the artist who obscures my view.
Thick acrylic makes it hard to see through.
 Here there is no brushing past.

There is only.
Me and you.

In a space where thin brushes break and our bodies
lie in stillness.
Ego floats above as we look below.
Shells filled with colour and texture.
 With no strokes to smooth the edges.

Our own art is us.

Messy hands as you wear stains on your sleeve.
Messy hands as we mix pallets and you become my primary colour.

SECTION 2:

TRAVEL

Body under a tube
Passengers get annoyed
There are now major delays

Ocean in Your Eyes

You left blank sheets whilst I scrawled through the air.
Traced the outlines of where your silhouette ceased to be.

Words curve past commas as you spill from my mouth.
The promise so mammoth my mind couldn't allow the ink to sink
With the fibres of you breath

Less.

Barriers brushed against my ankles as you anchored me to the bed.

I asked to see depth when you were blue.
But anger waved through you

And I crashed.

CRACKER

There's a woman eating crackers on the bus.
Why would you eat crackers?
They're dry with no topping.
But she's having a great time, crunching away.
The busses here tell you where to go.
How funny.
A talking bus.
A thing of childhood.
But we're so far into the future we don't see it.
Consumed by bright screens bending vertebrae we've been too busy
to notice.
Too cloudy to consider how far we've come.
I'm on a talking bus for fuck sake.
This bus knows more about where I'm going than I do.
That is a tragedy.
An African man keeps kissing his teeth: culture.
An old white couple converse with wirey hair.
Then towards the front there's two teens filled with exhaustion, a
small child in tow.
Struggle swimming through eyes.
They'll be okay.
The lady eating crackers is trying to do it low key.
She's got crackers in a white plastic bag.
The kind of bag you get food in from a market stall or a local green
grocers.
A market where they sell things you can't get in Tesco.
You'll hear the occasional crunch over the kissing of teeth, over the
breeze, over the talking bus.
And all these things make us move.
Make the wavelengths move in ways they've never and I sit amongst
it.
Panicked and comfortably cold.
Panicked knowing none of these things are under my control.
I cry knowing I'm lonely.
I laugh knowing I'm on a talking bus in London Town, Kent,
sitting going to Sunny Sidcup.

Travelling towards home?

The woman just rolled a chewing gum between her fingers.
Sticky wale fat in brown hands.

Absence when I get there.
Cry out and try and cast out loneliness, like some sort of spiritual
shamanism.
Not sure if that's the right word but I read it somewhere so that's
okay.
I forgot to order the book about personality disorders.

Personal disorder.

I'm getting off the stop after Suffolk Road.
You walk and you know.
Never has been.
Ended the way you didn't want.

Run to see.
Cry not to.

CRUNCH

Sometimes you've just gotta smile through it all haven't you. Really hard. Smile until it feels like your teeth will break & your gums will bleed till the bone of the tooth forces its way inside you like you did me. And don't get me wrong I'm trying my best not to be the most depressing cunt you've ever met.... yet here we are ey. However many minutes in. I've noticed Some people have laughed where I've cried. Where I've sat and cried whilst writing you've sat & laughed whilst watching, but I guess that's objectivity. I am the object of your eye. Or Apple if you're into that sort of thing. Sometimes it's easier to be hurt than to let go. It's like your wall climbing & the frog at the top holds the rope, who toads the line here? Get it? Yeah I know it's a shit joke, my therapist calls it a defence mechanism. I call it funny. Anyway the point is you're trying to scale this wall but your back is aching and your hands are burning from the rope. But you see this lovely green figurine at the top of it all, looking down, beaming up at you with love. And this hurts like a bitch but you've got to get to the top somehow. How'd you even get here in the first place? I think it's chronological... So far? There's a creak in the chair & you hope it splits & spits you into the fucking abyss.

OFF BALANCE

That night I taught you to dance in St Anne's square.
I danced all night wanting to be a different person in the morning.
Hoping it would bring you back.
When there are no words I can only explain through movement.
I saw youth in your eyes.
If anything I hope I left leaving you with that.
The lightness, airiness of laughter.
I hope I 'd left you with youth as you age.
But you knew that already.
Maybe in fleeting moments of the months that pass after me.
But youth in its bright and cheerful step all the same.

SECTION 3:

SWEET AND SKIN

I wish normal things would happen to me so I could be a person.
I think you don't want to chat to me.
That's why I'm scared to call.

SOFT WOOD

I'm an empty coffin in an hotel room.
Stiff as you sand me down, splintering
As you nail me. Your greasy lips against my skin.

'Would you like some chips?' you said.
It seemed Inappropriate to ask.
There were no thanks. Sirens

Made the room seem quieter.
I couldn't live with the fact
I could still smell chip fat

                           underneath my skin.

I'm your empty coffin. In a hotel room.
Buried beneath you.
Grounded to your earth.

Naked.

The same four walls. The same sweat.
I've only just seen it now.
Without the vulnerability this time.
Last time you cradled me as I shook.
As the Valium left my system.
Refusing to open double doors.
We ran and there was sweat.
And we were topless.
Then unclothed,
Not quite
Not quite
Then unclothed,
And we were topless.
We ran and there was sweat.
Refusing to open double doors.
As the Valium left my system.
Last time you cradled me as I shook.
Without the vulnerability this time.
I've only just seen it now.
The same four walls. The same sweat.

KAI

I'm so confused. Today it's strong, really strong the feeling of wanting a chest and a dick. To feel my chest pressing against another guys. To be part of that world that culture. To be seen as male. Today it's strong and I don't know what to do with it. I'm scared and I feel sick all at the same time, I don't know who to tell. Or if it's worth telling, or if it's just another day where my masculinity is taking over. Sometimes I feel free in my own skin & other days I feel bound. I want you to see me as male, feel me as male touch me as male - on some days more than others. Today especially. How do you know if it's fluidity or more - how the fuck are you supposed to know? I feel sick & I'm so scared, I'm so scared & I feel like I need to explore this further but I don't know how. It feels like I'm tryna' figure out my sexuality all over again. And then there's that thing that gender is just - it's not a proper thing, is it? I don't feel uncomfortable in this body but sometimes I want a boys body. I'd prefer a male body. There's an appeal.. There's strength, there's a flat chest, a deeper voice, guys fucking guys, getting with guys and I'm so far from that. Today it's a lot. Today it's a lot and it's heavy and I don't know what to do. Or who to tell or what's right or wrong or anything. Confusion is the worst state.

A Friday Fuck up

Right now I feel like, like the biggest pain in my chest. I want it to stop, really bad. I called a helpline and they didn't answer... I was on hold for a long time. I just want someone to tell me how to make the hurt stop. It comes in the quiet moments. Unaware. When I'm brushing my teeth or just sat on the tram. I want someone to tell me I should stay & how to make it stop. We all know what it's about by now. How the story goes. A person I know says sometimes I'm too abstract. Says the audience might not understand. Misunderstand. I keep thinking this is all one big misunderstanding. My brain replays the same moments to try & convince me it's real. I know it happened but I can't digest it. Hungover with hurt & its leaving me with headaches. I know I don't always make sense. But no one's asking you to make sense of it. No one's asking you for anything. You gave yourself that responsibility not me.

Skin

Four small walls. And, well, two people. Or beings, like bodies really. Skin. That's it, mainly just skin. Skin placed within four walls. Space. I gave it that, time and space for him to figure it out. I mean after our last embrace the hourglass of sand seemed to outline his face, you know move past it at a faster pace. I began to do that thing, forgetting. It was for the better really. But just as I couldn't picture him any more, there we were skin and friction and sweat. As we fucked. It began to slowly sink in. As he poured his sin onto my surfaces. The timer became full. We knew what we were doing. This was it, all this time had lead to this. Waiting. But waiting really long. Longing really hard and then finally, the anticipation was. Gone. And it was. It was needed. No emotion. No attachment. It was fucking. Fuck-ing in the rawest sense: mindless, sweaty the sort of sex that says 'Fuck you', the kind of feeling that's burning. You didn't know it was there, yearning to hurt each other in the best way that we could. In the backs of our minds we knew we could never be. So we took it out on one another physically. Don't get me wrong it wasn't scary or anything like that, it was filled to the brim with rage, like writing a strongly worded letter, but the words spill from the page. The occasional slap across the face. I slapped him back. A cheeky grin came across his face. Then something changed a different pace. Smashed my skin against the black wall. It was cold, really fucking cold, bit of a shock to the system you know. But it made me all the more present, only then, in that time, that place. Only then could it have happened. There was a mirror in there to you know, a full body mirror, but it's like there was no consciousness in our heads which could have lead us to being self-conscious, or conscious of one another. It was just a reflection of a feeling. A reflection of being human, alive. I know this sounds a bit, well, hard to understand, but I just want you to, think for a moment. Think about the feeling. Of feeling. The first time you fucked. Not when you lost your virginity or had sex. When you fucked. The intensity of it, the phenomenon that your never actually closer to someone than in that moment. It's gone now, our bodies an imprint, on a bed, surrounded by four walls. Surrounded by sweat. And then there it was again, accept without the vulnerability this time, I lay my head on his chest because we fucked. I lay my head on his chest because I felt him.

I felt everything that was wrong and saw it through the rage in his eyes. I felt feeling through the surface of his skin. It's amazing really, all that followed by breath. Cigarettes and a sweaty chest. I think in these moments we appreciate you know, being present. They'll always be there, feelings, whether it be fucking, or love, or hate. And that, well that's.....amazing.

SILENT

I asked for the time. You told me you didn't have it. Not at the beginning but the middle of the minute, seconds upon seconds within. All you had to say is that you didn't have it from the first second. Moment. As soon as the hands moved together and crossed paths. Touched. But it proved that even that was too much. It's something I've grown to loathe. That sense of need. Following the attachment. And we used to talk on the phone for hours. You stopped texting. Talking. So I stopped asking. You told me I was everything. I stood. You held me. You held me. You held me. But you wouldn't step forward as we stood on the edge of that cliff. You wouldn't bring me back onto the ledge. Instead you stood smoking as I slipped into the waves, feeling the pull against my face. This was it. I wanted to stay here. Feeling the pull and remembering the safety of your arms. I stopped asking. I stopped asking. I stopped asking. The hours of us passed, I stopped existing and I wasn't everything. A feeling which felt forever, but amounted to nothing. I broke your rose tints and you'll never forgive me. I was really fucking bad for you. But I'm still sorry we stopped.

SECTION 4:

SPACES

Sank into the ground
Surrounded by the city
Polluted but you were pure.

SURFACE

I.
Sometimes you're not sure are you.
Sometimes you sit in silence.
They avoid eye contact.
You touch and plea for something.
Anything.
Silence.
Between clicks of talking to others.
I'm here.
You worry you're not enough and that
Someone else is making them happier.
Someone else it making them smile and laugh more than you do.
You're filled with dread.
A word I don't use lightly.

Complete and absolute dread.

II.
Useless body.
Something to be talked about.
The head piece has been especially heavy today.
Screaming all sorts of shit.
I want a hug.
Exhausted and wanting someone to tell it to.
Attempting to pull myself up.
Pulling vertebrae by strings.
Thinner than fingers and easier broken.
Eat more-less-this-that.

Be a delay to the passengers, a burden to strangers, a burden to
loved ones.

Strangling in my sleep.

TOO FAR

I used the tone of the space.
I wish I could write my name in it
a thousand times in fine liner.
I'm off the ride but walking.
It feels confused. Almost static,
like touching the edge of grey blur
but reaching too far and falling into a channel on the TV screen.

Someone will relate. Someone will relate.
I feel like an artist with the wrong paintbrush.
I speak what I feel not toying with the words.
I don't paint with reds and blues.

And when he touches me I hope it doesn't feel
like nails against a chalkboard.

Be There

Me and this keyboard
and silence.

Except the words crowding my mind
like a busy street in town.
Silence.

Then people passing through, passing by.
She waved, but he didn't want to say goodbye.
I wish you hadn't changed.
His stillness turned to silence,

she kept the image in mind
of him fucking Jack and expecting her pride.
Instead all she felt was sickness,

and the sway of the words tipping the image into something else.
She felt sickness.

Touching his cheek his face smudged like a damp canvas
and it reminded her of soggy sandwiches at weddings, or worse:
funerals.
She felt sickness. Silence.

Except a smudged image in mind in a busy street in town.
Silence. Sickness.

He stood.

Guilt smudged across his face.

ARCTIC

Autumn is my favourite time of year to run.
Sort of dangerous because it's slippy, usually wet and the airs crisp
but not cold.
Enough to make you feel something, or numb depending on what
you're looking for.

What are you looking for? What are you doing here?
I ran till it hurt, until I could feel the feeling.
The crisp, then the numb.

Smiling a bit, dancing and getting caught by passing cars.
Singing and catching yourself smile.
It's like you rid of the motion sickness of missing home and
replaced it with movement through every bone.

My hands are sort of cold.
I like it.

Sort of dangerous because it's slippy and I can't stop thinking about
what you said to me.

21 percent battery and I'm lost.
Ran and walked in the same direction.
I'm not looking for anything.
Just love me.

I get why it makes you feel the way it does
It's got a kick to it
A beat.

Blurry white lights and speckled wet glass.
Soft, hard grass.
Flashing lights.

You're my emergency.
The bite.
And then the weightlessness.

ABANDONED

An endless conveyor of shit. Physical shit. A dripfeed of negative thoughts, feeding the brain and starving the body. If you can't respond in the same city how can you do it somewhere else? Force fed to eat. That's the last point, the last stand. Fake hospital for filming becomes the real thing. There's no full body mirror to tell me how bad it's getting. No reflection of self loathing to trust in. Trust what others tell you and remember how far it's gotten you. I wonder if someone told the anorexic women in ASDA she was anorexic, I wonder if anyone cared enough…Let's be fair here though. Let's think… no one really cares enough. There's got to be a cut off point where they go 'Fuck this I'm sick of hearing about your shit now'… Some people are just a big ball of 'shit' eventually, so much so you don't see who they used to be and they don't know who they used to be either. Consumed and clouded by walls, built brick by brick, slow and tireless blocking everyone out. So that's that, people get tired of constantly breaking down the 'wall' over and over, they give up and decide it's a waste of time and it's better to focus on themselves. Natural selfishness. No matter how much they love, or care, or want, or need, or how much you've changed, developed, loved that person. They'll always have that natural selfishness which is the cut off point. People are naturally selfish - anomie. Learned that one in Sociology, Anomie is the natural form of selfish human greed which we all have living underneath our skin. So when it gets to a specific point, it's like they wake up and remember you're not important and move on. They move on, along with the conveyor belt of shit. Everybody wave bye bye.

Have you ever felt the type of exhaustion that if you take one more train ride you'll flop onto the tracks. Sounds nice, comfortable, like a comfy not to firm sort of bed. But it's hard and cold, metallic. Like the people. Like the concrete of London. The robot people would blow out steam if it happened. If you actually did it. Angered at another train delay. You've ruined their day now. Shit. Always making things worse. Could you actually imagine. Don't. You don't have to. The tin men of London town will tell you of many inconveniences where train rides have been delayed on account of a floppy body on the tracks. Recon you could hear the bones crunch? Or is that too graphic for you. Sorry. Sometimes I have to stop to wipe the snot from my face because I cry so much. A fireplace sits in front of me with no fire. More of a chimney. A brick wall feature in a brick wall room where assault took place. Casual? I just told you an assault took place. Casual. That sort of crying didn't have snot. More of a helpless scream, plead, whimper. Like an animal being forcefully impregnated. Makes me want to be a vegan. Experiencing first hand. The first hand you trust to touch again also becomes the first hand to take it away. First hand, then mouth, then... You know the rest. Too much? Sit back, enjoy the ride, there's more to come. Who said this was a good idea?

It's rush hour in my mind and there's no red lights.

ABOUT SUPERBIA BOOKS

This book was one of three winners of the Superbia Chapbook Competition. The prize was funded by Manchester Pride, and the three winning entries comprise the debut publications under the Superbia Books imprint of Dog Horn Publishing. All three chapbooks will be launched as part of Manchester Pride's Superbia strand of arts and cultural events in Greater Manchester.

Additional funding was provided by Commonword in order to mentor the writers, prepare them for publication and organise launch events. Commonword is the literature development agency for the North West.

The editing and mentoring was undertaken by Adam Lowe on behalf of Young Enigma. Founded with seed money from Commonword, Young Enigma supports young and emerging writers from Manchester and the North West.

Find out more at superbia.org.uk, cultureword.org.uk and youngenigma.com.

SUPERBIA CHAPBOOK WINNERS

A Creature of Transformation, James Hodgson
19 Years of Skin, Kenya Sterling
Vivat Regina, Maz Hedgehog

ND - #0182 - 270225 - C0 - 229/152/2 - PB - 9781907133206 - Matt Lamination